SCIENCE STORY LIBRARY

Young children can grasp scientific concepts and are interested in the world they live in. The Science Story Library is designed to answer this interest. The books present important scientific events and tell the lives of great men of science. They offer concepts meaningful to children through good—and scientifically accurate —storytelling. The series is illustrated by leading American artists.

BENJAMIN FRANKLIN, SCIENTIST–DIPLOMAT
By Charles Michael Daugherty / Illustrated by John Falter

ROBERT GODDARD, TRAIL BLAZER TO THE STARS
By Charles Michael Daugherty / Illustrated by James Daugherty

ARCHIMEDES, MATHEMATICIAN AND INVENTOR
By Martin Gardner / Illustrated by Leonard Everett Fisher

GALILEO GALILEI, SPACE PIONEER
By Arthur S. Gregor / Illustrated by James W. Williamson

SIGMUND FREUD, DOCTOR OF SECRETS AND DREAMS
By John Mann / Illustrated by Clare Romano Ross and John Ross

SIR ARTHUR EVANS, DISCOVERER OF KNOSSOS
By George Selden / Illustrated by Lee Ames

HEINRICH SCHLIEMANN, DISCOVERER OF BURIED TREASURE
By George Selden / Illustrated by Lorence F. Bjorklund

ALEXANDER THE GREAT, SCIENTIST–KING
By Robert C. Suggs / Illustrated by Leonard Everett Fisher

MATHEMATICIAN
AND INVENTOR

ARCHIMEDES

BY
MARTIN GARDNER

ILLUSTRATED BY
LEONARD EVERETT FISHER

THE MACMILLAN COMPANY, NEW YORK
COLLIER-MACMILLAN LIMITED, LONDON

The Macmillan Company, New York
Collier-Macmillan Canada, Ltd., Toronto, Ontario
Library of Congress catalog card number: 65-10176
Printed in the United States of America
First Printing

U. S. 1321928

▣▣ ARCHIMEDES ▣▣
MATHEMATICIAN AND INVENTOR

MORE than two thousand years ago a fat, jolly king named Hiero II was the ruler of Syracuse, a beautiful city on the island of Sicily, then primarily a Greek possession.

One day the king's jeweler, who was skilled in making all kinds of things out of gold, brought him a new crown. The king put it on and admired himself in a mirror.

"What a handsome king am I!" he exclaimed, smiling.

After the goldsmith had left, King Hiero took off his new gold crown and held it in his hand. "Hmmm," he said to himself. "Gold is a heavy metal but this crown seems almost as light as silver. I wonder if my goldsmith has tried to make a fool of me by mixing some silver with the gold. I don't trust him."

The king sent for his good friend Archimedes, a

famous scientist who lived in Syracuse. "You are very good at solving problems, Archimedes," said the king, who was wise as well as fat and jolly. "I want to know if this new crown of mine is really made of pure gold. Is there some way you can test it for me?" (Today it is easy to find out if objects are made of pure gold by testing them with certain chemicals. But in Archimedes' time no one knew about such tests.)

"It is a difficult problem, dear King," said Archimedes.

"Doesn't gold weigh more than silver?" the king asked.

"It does, Your Majesty."

"Then," said the king, "why can't you just weigh my crown and see if it weighs as much as the same amount of gold?"

Archimedes smiled. "To do that, we would first have to measure the crown to find out exactly how much metal is in it."

"Well, measure it, then," said the king impatiently.

Archimedes shook his head. "Impossible. The shape is much too complicated. The only way we could measure it would be to hammer it into the shape of a small gold block. And then, of course, we'd have to measure the block."

The king looked horrified. "But that would ruin my beautiful new crown!"

"It would indeed," replied Archimedes. "We must find a way to test your crown without destroying it. Let me think about it for a while."

After Archimedes left the palace, he walked slowly along the streets of Syracuse. He came to a bath-house. In those days people went to public bath-houses—just as some peoples do today—instead of having bathtubs in their homes.

Archimedes decided to go inside and take a bath, still thinking about a way to test the crown. This particular problem fascinated the scientist. He knew there must be an answer. He lay back and relaxed. He could feel the water pushing up on his body, making him feel very light in weight.

Suddenly Archimedes thought of a simple way to test the crown. He could weigh it in the air, and weigh it in water. Then, by using mathematics, he could tell whether the crown was pure gold. (If you want to find out exactly how he did this, turn to page 40.)

Archimedes was so excited that he completely forgot he was taking a bath. He leaped up and, without a stitch of clothing on, ran through the streets of Syracuse shouting "Eureka! Eureka!"

Do you know what "eureka" means? It is an ancient Greek word meaning "I have found it." This story about Archimedes is so well known that even today when someone solves a difficult problem he sometimes shouts "Eureka!"

We do not know whether Archimedes found the crown of pure gold or whether the goldsmith had cheated the king. That part of the story has been forgotten. But we do know that this was one of the first truly great experiments in science.

Archimedes made many other experiments with objects in water. He was the first to explain why a stone weighs less if you hold it under water, and why a cork pops to the surface if you hold it under water and let go.

This scientist was also the first to use mathe-

matics in solving important scientific problems. His father had been an astronomer. Greek scientists who studied the stars were skilled in calculating with numbers, so it was probably from his father that Archimedes first learned about mathematics. As a young man he went to Egypt, a country to the southeast of Sicily, on the continent of Africa, to study mathematics at a famous school in the city of Alexandria. After he had completed his studies, he came back to Syracuse where he lived for the rest of his life.

Archimedes loved mathematics more than anything else in the world. On cold winter nights when
he sat by the fire, he would rake out the ashes so he
could draw triangles and other geometric figures in
them. It was the custom of the ancient Greeks to rub
oil on their bodies after they bathed. When Archimedes did this he liked to use the tip of his finger
for drawing figures on his oily skin. He thought
about mathematics when he went to bed at night.
He thought about mathematics when he got up in
the morning and sometimes he was so busy thinking
about mathematics that he would forget to eat his
dinner!

Archimedes was not only a great scientist and mathematician, he was also a great inventor. He made experiments with simple devices such as levers, pulleys, and cogwheels that move and turn other wheels. By using these devices in clever ways, he was able to build many different kinds of machines that no one had ever built before.

One of his most famous inventions was a pump for making water flow uphill. The picture shows how it works. The pipe is coiled around a cylinder in the same way that a red stripe coils around a candy cane or a barber's pole. When the man turns the cylinder with his feet, the low end of the pipe dips into the water. As the cylinder turns, water is carried up through the pipe until it flows out the other end. This simple pump is called the *screw of Archimedes.* It was used for hundreds of years in Egypt and other parts of the ancient world to lift water from a low river or lake up to higher ground where it is needed for farming. In some parts of the world farmers still use it today.

Another of Archimedes' remarkable inventions was a small planetarium, a model for showing how the planets move. Balls of different sizes were used to represent the earth, sun, moon, and the five planets—Mercury, Venus, Mars, Jupiter, and Saturn —that were known in ancient times. When a crank was turned, the balls would move around the earth just the way they appear to move across our sky at night. Archimedes could even demonstrate eclipses of the sun and moon. With his model planetarium he could show how the sun would at times be covered by the moon when it passed between the sun and the earth, and how the moon would at various times be hidden by the shadow of the earth.

One sunny afternoon, when Archimedes and King
Hiero were strolling through the royal gardens, they
came upon some children on a seesaw. A seesaw is
really a simple lever. Archimedes tried to explain to
the king how such a lever could be used for lifting
heavy things.

"If one end of a seesaw is very long," Archimedes said, "and the other end very short, you could put an elephant on the short end, then lift him high in the air by pushing down on the long end."

"Amazing!" exclaimed the king.

"With science one can do even more amazing things," said Archimedes. "In fact, if I had a lever that was long enough and strong enough, and there was a place for me to stand, I could lift the entire world!" (This is Archimedes' best-remembered remark, and one President Kennedy repeated in a speech made to the United Nations.)

King Hiero laughed so hard at Archimedes' boast that his gold crown fell off and rolled on the grass. "Come now, dear friend, you can't expect me to believe that."

"I mean every word," said Archimedes. "No object is so big that it can't be moved, if only you have the right machine to do the job."

The king thanked Archimedes for picking up and returning his crown. He pointed with it toward the blue sea sparkling in the sunlight, where one of his largest ships was anchored. "Can you make a machine that will move that ship through the water? It weighs more than a hundred elephants."

Archimedes said nothing, but he smiled to himself as he tugged on his beard and thought about the king's ship.

A few days later Archimedes asked the king to meet him at a spot on the shore near the ship. A long rope was fastened to the front of the ship. The rope stretched across the quiet water to the rocky shore where it was attached to a strange-looking machine made of many wheels.

"Your Majesty," said Archimedes, "I have prepared this demonstration to prove to you the great power of science. Please turn the crank on that machine."

King Hiero did as he was told. When he turned the crank the machine's wheels began to squeak and spin around. Soon the heavy three-masted ship, loaded with sailors and supplies, was moving slowly through the water toward the shore.

The king was so impressed by this demonstration that he turned to speak to a crowd of people who had gathered around to watch. "From now on," he said to them, "anything Archimedes says must be believed."

King Hiero persuaded Archimedes to invent many different kinds of machines that could be used in fighting wars. These machines were built, but never used by Hiero because he was wise and kind, and knew how to live in peace with his neighbors. But when Archimedes was an old man, and Hieronymus, a grandson of Hiero, had become king, a bitter war broke out. From Rome, the great city in Italy which ruled over many other cities, a famous general named Marcellus set sail for Syracuse with sixty ships and many soldiers. He intended to land his men on the shore just outside the city's walls, so that he could invade the city and put it under Roman rule.

"We need your help, Archimedes," said the worried young king. "We still have all those strange-looking machines you built for my grandfather. One of them, I remember, is a big mirror that looks like a giant saucer. Will you teach us how to use these machines?"

Archimedes would have preferred to spend his time working on mathematical problems, but he knew that his city was in great danger, so he bowed low before the king, and said: "I will show you how to use the machines, Your Majesty."

When the Roman ships arrived at Syracuse, Marcellus turned to one of his men. "This will be an easy victory," he said. "The Syracusans are rich and lazy. They know nothing about how to fight a war."

But Archimedes was ready. He had the king's men put the big mirror on top of one of the high towers of the palace. It caught the rays of the bright, hot sun and focused them on the nearest of the Roman ships. Suddenly the wooden ship caught fire and began to burn!

The Greeks turned the mirror and aimed the sun's rays at another ship. It too caught fire!

Marcellus ordered his ships to turn back. He was furious. "That mirror must be one of Archimedes' inventions," he said to the captain of his ship. "But it is useless without the sun. We will wait until the sun is behind the clouds, then we will try again to land our men."

But Archimedes had other machines waiting. When a Roman ship sailed close to the high wall that ran along the shore, a long pole was suddenly pushed out from the top of the wall. An enormous boulder fastened to its end was carried across the water until it was directly above the ship. The boulder was released.

Crash! The huge rock smashed the front end of the ship. It tore a big hole in the ship's bottom. The ship began to sink! The Romans now knew that Hieronymus was well prepared for battle.

Another enormous pole appeared. This one had a gigantic iron hook on its end. It hooked into the side of a ship and quickly flipped it upside down!

Still another pole! An iron claw on the end of the third pole gripped the stern, or back end, of a ship and lifted it high into the air. It shook the ship from side to side until all the men tumbled into the sea! The empty ship was carried over to the rocky shore and dropped. It smashed into a thousand pieces.

The Roman soldiers and sailors on the other ships turned pale, and shook with fright. What new and terrible war machine would Archimedes try next? It seemed to them, as one ancient writer put it, as if they were fighting not against men but against the gods. Marcellus ordered his ships to turn around and sail away as fast as they could.

For three years the terrible war machines of Archimedes kept Marcellus and his army from capturing the city. U. S. 1321928

But Marcellus was a clever general. One night he landed his men secretly at another spot on the island of Sicily. He waited until the Syracusans were having a big holiday celebration in honor of their goddess Diana. Everyone had stuffed himself with food, drunk many cups of wine, and gone sound asleep. When they awoke the next morning, their beloved city had been taken. Its streets echoed with the shouts of Roman soldiers.

Marcellus had come to have great respect for
Archimedes. He knew that Archimedes was the
greatest scientist then living—perhaps the greatest
who had ever lived. "Find him and bring him to

me," he told his men. "But be gentle. He is an old man. See that he is not harmed in any way."

The soldiers went to look for Archimedes. One of them found him busy at work on a mathematical problem. In working on problems, Greek mathematicians did not have blackboards and chalk, or pencils and paper. They had wooden boards covered with fine loose sand. With a stick, or the tip of a finger, they would write numbers and draw shapes in the sand. To erase, they used the palms of their hands to smooth the sand evenly over the board again.

Archimedes was drawing circles on his sand board when the dark shadow of a Roman soldier fell across

the sand. "Please move away," Archimedes said. "I am very busy."

"You must come with me," replied the soldier. He was annoyed by this stubborn, white-bearded old man who hardly gave him a second glance.

"I can't go with you now," Archimedes said firmly. "Kindly go away and leave me alone."

The soldier lost his temper. He drew his sharp sword and plunged it through the defenseless old man—without stopping to think what Marcellus would say.

Archimedes was seventy-five years old when this cruel warrior killed him. He might have lived years longer and made many more great discoveries. The time was 212 B.C., which means 212 years before the birth of Christ. The Romans were not much interested in science and mathematics, and more than a thousand years were to go by before there were any scientists as great as Archimedes.

The world has long ago forgotten the name of that hot-tempered Roman soldier. It hardly remembers the names of King Hiero and Marcellus, the general.

But the name of Archimedes has never been forgotten. Today, in every country, his great discoveries are known and his name is honored.

This is what Archimedes did to find out whether the king's crown was pure gold or not:

1. First he weighed a lump of gold he knew was pure.

2. Then he weighed the same lump of gold suspended in water. Because water presses *up* on the gold, the gold weighs less than it does in air.

3. He subtracted the weight of the gold in water from its weight in air. The difference between the two weights is the same as the weight of that amount of water displaced by the gold lump. This difference is equal to the force with which the water presses up on the gold.

4. He divided the weight of the gold in air by the amount of weight it *lost* when it was in water (that is, by the difference obtained in Step 3). The result is what today is called the *specific gravity* of gold. It is 19.3. This number is *always the same, no matter what shape or size the gold is.* It can be a small gold ring or a large

gold crown. If it is pure gold, the weight in air divided by the loss of weight in water will always be 19.3. This procedure may be used to determine the specific gravity of any solid material.

Do you see how Archimedes could test the crown?

Actually, it was very simple: all he had to do was to repeat what he had done with the lump of gold, using the crown instead of the lump.

1. He weighed the crown in air.

2. He weighed the crown in water.

3. He divided the weight of the crown in air by its loss of weight in water. Then he compared the answer with the answer for the lump of gold. If it was 19.3, the specific gravity of gold, he would know that the crown was pure gold. If it was less than 19.3, he would know that the gold had been mixed with a lighter-weight metal such as silver. (Silver has a specific gravity of 10.5.)

ABOUT THE AUTHOR: Martin Gardner was born in Tulsa, Oklahoma, in 1914. He received a Bachelor of Arts degree from the University of Chicago, where he majored in philosophy. During World War II he spent four years in the Navy and traveled around the world. Since the war, Mr. Gardner has been a free-lance writer and was a contributing editor to *Humpty Dumpty's Magazine for Little Children* for eight years. Two of his most widely known books are: *Science Puzzlers* and *Mathematical Puzzles.* Mr. Gardner lives in Hastings-on-Hudson with his wife and two sons.

ABOUT THE ILLUSTRATOR: Leonard Everett Fisher has illustrated more than a hundred books for young people. A native of New York, he studied art at the Heckscher Foundation, the Art Students League, and the studio of Moses Soyer. He received two degrees in fine arts from Yale University. The Library of Congress has acquired some of his illustrations, his paintings have been included in national shows, and he received a Pulitzer traveling fellowship. Mr. Fisher has also illustrated *Alexander the Great, Before Adam, The Star Rover, The Weigher of Souls and The Earth Dwellers* for Macmillan. He and his family live in Westport, Connecticut.